MASTERING THE ESSENTIALS: NAVIGATING MICROSOFT EXCEL INTERFACE AND CORE FUNCTIONS

This topic emphasizes guiding novices through the Excel interface while providing an approachable introduction to its foundational features. The preliminary course content covers:

- Overview of Excel Interface: Explaining the layout, ribbon, toolbar, and worksheet navigation.
- Workbook and Worksheet Concepts: Understanding workbooks, worksheets, and their practical uses.
- Cell Basics: Entering, editing, and formatting data in cells.
- Introduction to Basic Formulas and Functions: Learning how to use common functions like SUM, AVERAGE, and basic calculations.
- Data Management: Introduction to sorting, filtering, and organizing data in Excel.
- Preliminary Hands-On Exercises: Basic tasks to reinforce learning, such as creating a simple budget or to-do list.

Contents

Overview of the Excel Interface: Explaining the Layout, Ribbon, Toolbar, and Worksheet Navigation

Microsoft Excel's interface is designed to help users efficiently create, manage, and analyze data. For beginners, understanding the layout, navigation, and key elements of Excel is crucial for working effectively with spreadsheets. This overview explains the various components of the Excel interface, including the ribbon, toolbar, and worksheet navigation, to build a solid foundation for working with Excel.

Excel Layout

When you open Excel, the main working area is divided into several key components. Each part of the interface has its own function, helping users manage data, apply formatting, and perform calculations efficiently.

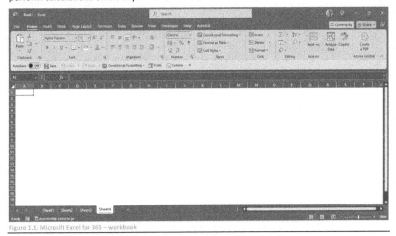

Figure 1.1: Microsift Excel for 365 – workbook

Workbook and Worksheet

Workbook: A workbook is the entire Excel file that contains one or more worksheets (also known as sheets). You can think of a workbook as a binder that holds multiple sheets.

Worksheet: A worksheet is a single spreadsheet within the workbook. It consists of a grid of cells arranged in rows and columns. You can have multiple worksheets within one workbook and switch between them easily.

Columns and Rows

Columns: These are vertical groups of cells, labeled alphabetically (A, B, C, etc.). After column Z, columns are labeled as AA, AB, and so on. Figure 2 shows the graphical illustration of a column.

Rows: These are horizontal groups of cells, labeled numerically (1, 2, 3, etc.). Rows and columns intersect to form cells. Figure 2 shows the graphical illustration of a row.

Cells

A cell is the basic unit in Excel where you enter data, formulas, or functions. It is basically the point at which a column intercept a row in excel. Each cell is identified by its cell reference, which is a combination of the column letter and row number (e.g., A1, B2, C3) that intercepted. When you select a cell, it becomes the active cell. Figure 2 shows the graphical illustration of a cell.

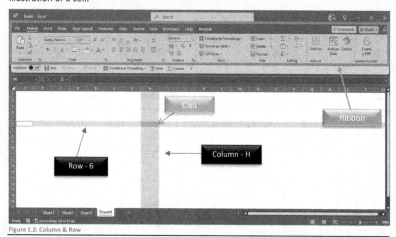

Figure 1.2: Column & Row

The Ribbon

The Ribbon is the toolbar at the top of the Excel window that contains tabs and commands for performing various tasks. It organizes all of Excel's tools into different groups, making them easy to find and use.

Tabs on the Ribbon

The Ribbon is divided into several tabs, each containing groups of related commands as detailed below:

❖ **Home**: This is the default tab that contains essential tools for formatting, aligning text, and managing cells. It includes group pf command for font styling, text alignment, number formatting, cell styles, and basic editing tasks like copy, paste, paint, and find/replace.

❖ **Insert**: This tab contains options to insert tables, pictures, charts, illustrations, links, and other objects into your worksheet. It also allows you to add headers, footers, and text boxes.

❖ **Draw**: This tab helps you to perform basic drawing function and to convert inks to shapes or maths.

❖ **Page Layout**: This tab helps you manage the layout and appearance of your worksheet, including margins, orientation (portrait or landscape), print areas, and themes.

❖ **Formulas**: This tab is where you'll find functions and tools for performing calculations. It includes categories for financial, logical, and statistical functions, as well as formula auditing tools and more recently Python (Preview)

- ❖ **Data**: This tab helps you manage data, with tools for sorting, filtering, validating, and importing data from external sources.
- ❖ *Review*: This tab is focused on proofreading and collaboration. It includes tools for adding comments, checking spelling, and protecting worksheets.
- ❖ **View**: This tab allows you to control how you view your worksheet. It includes options for zooming, freezing panes, switching between different workbooks, and managing window layouts.
- ❖ *Contextual Tabs*: In addition to the standard tabs, contextual tabs appear when you select certain objects, such as charts or tables. These tabs provide specific tools for formatting or managing the selected object.

Figure 1.3: Tabs

Ribbon Groups

Each tab is divided into groups of related commands. For example, In the Home tab, you'll find groups like Clipboard, Font, Alignment, Number, styles, cells and editing.

Each group contains buttons, drop-down menus, and dialog box launchers that open additional settings for more advanced options.

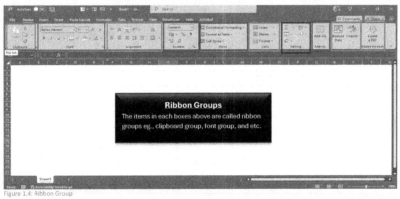

Figure 1.4: Ribbon Group

Collapsing and Expanding the Ribbon

To maximize workspace, you can collapse or expand the ribbon:

❖ **Collapse**: Click the small arrow icon at the top-right corner of the ribbon or press Ctrl + F1.

❖ **Expand**: Click the arrow again or press Ctrl + F1 to bring the ribbon back.

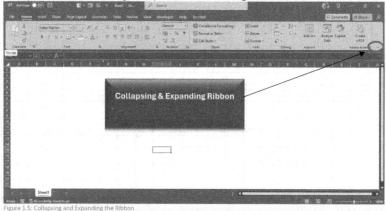

Figure 1.5: Collapsing and Expanding the Ribbon

Quick Access Toolbar

The Quick Access Toolbar (QAT) is a customizable toolbar located at the top of the Excel window, above the Ribbon. It provides quick access to frequently used commands, such as Save, Undo, Redo, and Print.

Customizing the Quick Access Toolbar: You can add or remove commands from the QAT by clicking the drop-down arrow next to it. This allows you to tailor the toolbar with your most-used features for easy access.

To add a command, select it from the list in the drop-down menu or click More Commands to choose from a wider selection.

You can also choose to display the QAT below the ribbon for easier access.

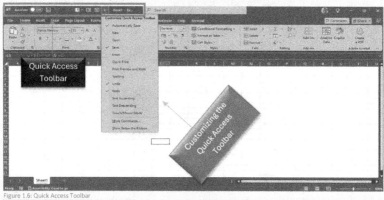

Figure 1.6: Quick Access Toolbar

Formula Bar

The Formula Bar is located just below the ribbon and is used to enter or edit data, formulas, or functions in the selected cell.

Cell Reference Box: On the left side of the formula bar, the cell reference box shows the location of the currently selected (active) cell.

Formula Entry Area: On the right side of the formula bar, you can enter data or formulas. If the selected cell contains a formula, the formula will be displayed here.

The formula bar allows you to easily edit complex formulas or review long text entries that may not fully display within a single cell.

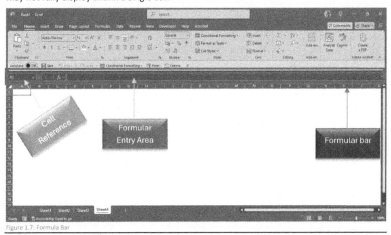

Figure 1.7: Formula Bar

Worksheet Tabs

At the bottom of the Excel window, you'll find worksheet tabs, which allow you to switch between different sheets within the workbook. Each tab represents a separate worksheet, and you can have multiple sheets in one workbook.

Adding and Managing Worksheets: To add a new worksheet, click the + button next to the worksheet tabs or press Shift + F11.

❖ You can *rename a worksheet* by double-clicking the sheet tab and entering a new name.
❖ To *move or copy a worksheet*, right-click on the sheet tab and choose Move or Copy.

Color-Coding Worksheet Tabs: To better organize your workbook, you can color-code worksheet tabs. Right-click on a tab, select Tab Color, and choose a color. This is helpful when working with complex workbooks containing multiple sheets.

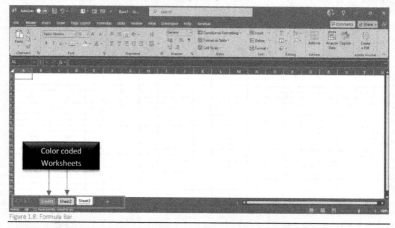

Figure 1.8: Formula Bar

Status Bar

The Status Bar is located at the bottom of the Excel window. It provides quick information about selected cells and allows for easy access to certain features.

Zoom Slider: You can use the zoom slider in the bottom-right corner to adjust the zoom level of your worksheet.

Basic Calculations: When you select a range of cells containing numbers, the status bar displays basic calculations like Sum, Average, and Count for the selected cells. You can customize which calculations are shown by right-clicking the status bar.

The status bar also shows important information, such as whether Caps Lock or Num Lock is active and which View Mode (Normal, Page Layout, or Page Break) you're currently in.

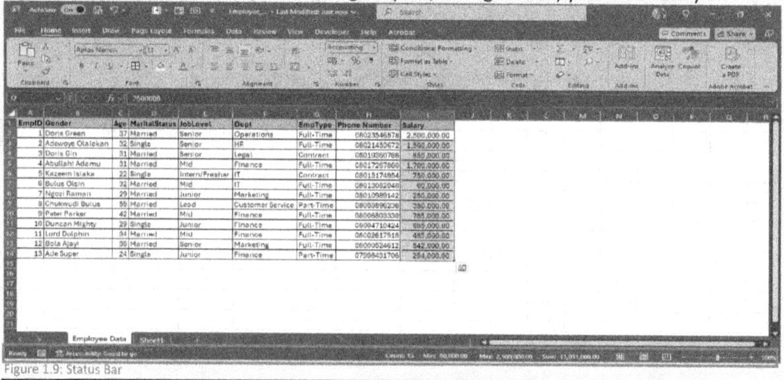

Figure 1.9: Status Bar

Navigation and Working with Worksheets

Excel provides several features to help you navigate large worksheets and multiple workbooks efficiently.

Scroll Bars:

You can use the vertical and horizontal scroll bars to move through your worksheet. These are especially useful when working with large datasets that extend beyond the visible area.

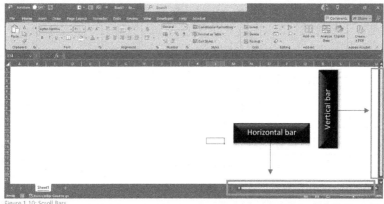

Figure 1.10: Scroll Bars

Freezing Panes

When working with large datasets, you can freeze panes to keep important rows or columns visible as you scroll through the worksheet.

❖ To freeze the top row (usually a header row), go to View tab >Windows group > Freeze Panes and select Freeze Top Row.
❖ To freeze the first column, choose Freeze First Column from the same menu.
❖ For custom freezing, select the row or column below and to the right of the data you want to freeze, then choose Freeze Panes.

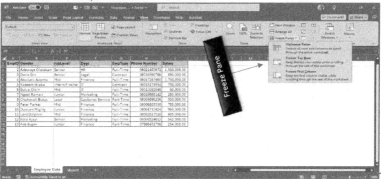

Figure 1.11: Freeze Pane

Keyboard Shortcuts:

FOR EDITING	FOR FORMATTING	FOR NAVIGATION:	FOR SELECTION:	FOR FORMULA AND DATA
F2: Edit the active cell.	**Ctrl + B**: Bold text.	**Arrow Keys**: Move one cell up, down, left, or right.	**Shift + Arrow Key** : Extend selection by one cell.	**Alt + =**: AutoSum selected cells.
Ctrl + X / C / V: Cut, Copy, and Paste	**Ctrl + I**: Italicize text.	**Ctrl + Arrow Key**: Jump to the edge of a data range in the direction of the arrow.	**Ctrl + Shift + Arrow Key**: Extend selection to the last non-empty cell.	**Ctrl + `**: Toggle between displaying formulas and results.
Ctrl + Z: Undo.	**Ctrl + U**: Underline text.	**Page Up/Page Down**: Move up or down one screen.	**Ctrl + A**: Select the entire dataset. Press again to select the entire sheet.	**Ctrl + T**: Convert a range into a table.
Ctrl + Y: Redo.	**Ctrl + 1**: Open the Format Cells dialog box.	**Ctrl + Page Up/Page Down**: Move between worksheet tabs.	**Shift + Space**: Select the entire row.	
Ctrl + D: Fill down (copy the cell above).	**Ctrl + Shift + $**: Apply currency format.	**Ctrl + Home**: Jump to the top-left corner of the worksheet (cell A1).	**Ctrl + Space**: Select the entire column.	
Ctrl + R: Fill right (copy the cell to the left).	**Ctrl + Shift + %**: Apply percentage format.	**Ctrl + End**: Jump to the last used cell in the worksheet.		
Ctrl + ;: Insert the current date.	**Ctrl + Shift +**: Apply date format.	**Ctrl + E**: Flash fill		
Ctrl + Shift + ;: Insert the current time.	**Ctrl + Shift + @**: Apply time format.			
Alt + Enter: Start a new line within the same cell.				

Table 1.1

Understanding the Excel interface is essential for efficiently managing data, performing calculations, and analyzing information. Mastering the Ribbon, Toolbar, Worksheet Tabs, and navigation features will enable users to work faster and more effectively in Excel.

2.

Workbook and Worksheet Concepts: Understanding Workbooks, Worksheets, and Their Practical Uses

In Microsoft Excel, workbooks and worksheets form the core structure for organizing, storing, and manipulating data. Grasping the distinction between these two elements and how they interact is essential for anyone working with Excel. This section will break down the concepts of workbooks and worksheets, explain their practical uses, and offer insights into how they contribute to effective data management.

What is a Workbook?

A workbook is an Excel file that contains one or more worksheets. Think of it as a container or a binder that holds related sheets of data. When you open Excel, you're opening a workbook, and when you save your work, you're saving the entire workbook, which can consist of multiple worksheets. Figure 1 above depicts a workbook.

Workbook Components:

File Format: A workbook is saved as a file with an extension such as .xlsx (default for modern Excel versions), .xls (for older versions), or .xlsm (for macro-enabled files).
Multiple Worksheets: A workbook can contain numerous worksheets (also called sheets), each with its own data and functions. These sheets can be used independently or linked to one another to perform more complex operations.

Practical Uses of Workbooks:

Project Management: You can keep multiple project-related data sheets (e.g., budget, timeline, resource allocation) in a single workbook for easy reference and management.

Financial Reporting: Businesses often use workbooks to compile financial statements such as balance sheets, income statements, and cash flow statements, each on different worksheets but stored together in one workbook.

Data Consolidation: When working with different datasets (e.g., sales data by region), you can keep each dataset on separate worksheets within the same workbook to easily consolidate and analyze them together.

What is a Worksheet?

A worksheet is a grid of rows and columns where you enter, organize, and manipulate data. When you open a new Excel workbook, you typically start with one blank worksheet, but you can add, delete, or rename worksheets as needed. See figure 8 above.

Key Features of a Worksheet:

Rows and Columns: A worksheet is made up of horizontal rows (numbered 1, 2, 3, etc.) and vertical columns (labeled A, B, C, etc.), forming a grid where data is entered into cells.

Cells: Each intersection of a row and a column creates a cell (e.g., A1, B2), which is the basic unit for storing data, formulas, or functions.

Cell Reference: Every cell has a unique address known as a cell reference, based on its row and column (e.g., C5 refers to the cell in column C and row 5). Refer to figure 2 above. The highlighted cell is **H6** (the interception between column H and row 6).

Practical Uses of Worksheets:

Organizing Data: A worksheet can be used to keep track of data, such as lists of contacts, inventory, sales figures, or survey results.

Performing Calculations: Worksheets allow users to perform complex calculations, from basic arithmetic to advanced statistical analysis, using formulas and functions.

Data Analysis: Worksheets are ideal for analyzing data, allowing you to sort, filter, create pivot tables, and apply conditional formatting to draw insights.

Charts and Visuals: Excel's worksheet space allows you to visualize data using charts, graphs, and other visual tools, making it easier to interpret large sets of numbers.

Workbook and Worksheet Interactions:

Understanding how workbooks and worksheets interact is critical for leveraging Excel's full potential. In most cases, multiple worksheets in a workbook are used to organize different but related data sets, while workbook-level operations provide a holistic view of all the data.

Linking Worksheets:

You can create links between different worksheets within the same workbook to refer to data across sheets. This is useful for creating summary sheets, pulling data from one sheet into another, or referencing data points without duplicating them.

Example: If Sheet1 contains sales data for January and Sheet2 contains sales data for February, you can create a third sheet to summarize total sales by pulling data from both sheets.

Formulas Across Worksheets:

Excel allows you to use formulas that reference cells or ranges from other worksheets. This enables more dynamic and comprehensive data analysis.

Example: In Sheet3, you could enter a formula like =Sheet1!A1 + Sheet2!A1, which sums the value in cell A1 of both Sheet1 and Sheet2.

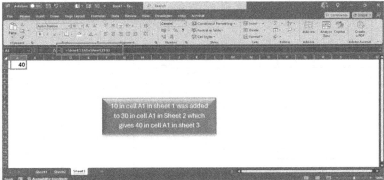

Figure 2.1: Formulas across worksheet

Consolidating Data:

Workbooks are commonly used to consolidate data from multiple worksheets. For example, you can have a different worksheet for each department in a company, and then use a master worksheet to consolidate department data into a comprehensive report.

Managing Workbooks and Worksheets
Adding and Removing Worksheets:

Adding Worksheets: You can add new worksheets to a workbook by clicking the + sign next to the sheet tabs at the bottom of the Excel window or by using the shortcut Shift + F11.

Deleting Worksheets: Right-click the worksheet tab and choose Delete to remove a sheet. Be careful when deleting, as this action cannot be undone.

Renaming Worksheets:

To keep your workbook organized, you should rename your worksheets based on their content. To do this, double-click the sheet tab and type the new name (e.g., "January Sales" or "Expenses").

Moving and Copying Worksheets:

You can rearrange the order of worksheets by dragging the sheet tab to the desired location. Additionally, right-clicking the sheet tab allows you to move or copy the worksheet to another location within the same workbook or even to a different workbook.

Color-Coding Worksheets:

Excel allows you to assign colors to worksheet tabs to make navigation easier, especially when working with multiple sheets. Right-click on the worksheet tab, select Tab Color, and choose your preferred color.

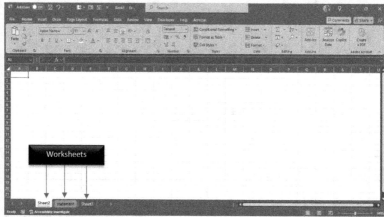

Figure 2.2: Workbook / worksheet management

Worksheet Protection:

To prevent unauthorized changes to your data, Excel offers worksheet protection. You can lock a worksheet to prevent editing of certain cells or the entire sheet by going to Review > Protect Sheet and setting a password.

Practical Applications of Workbooks and Worksheets

Workbooks and worksheets are flexible tools for a variety of real-world tasks, ranging from personal projects to complex business operations.

Budget Planning:

You can create a workbook to manage personal or organizational budgets. Each worksheet can represent different aspects of the budget, such as income, expenses, and savings goals.

Example: One worksheet could track income sources, while another logs monthly expenses. A summary worksheet could display the overall budget, pulling data from the other sheets.

Project Tracking:

For project management, a workbook can contain worksheets for tracking tasks, timelines, resources, and progress.

Example: A project manager might create separate sheets for different phases of a project, with each worksheet tracking specific tasks and timelines, while a summary sheet gives an overall view of the project's status.

Sales and Inventory Management:

A workbook is useful for keeping track of sales and inventory. One worksheet can be dedicated to recording daily sales, another for inventory levels, and a third for sales analysis and forecasting.

Example: By linking the sales sheet to the inventory sheet, you can automatically update stock levels as sales occur, helping maintain accurate records.

Data Analysis and Reporting:

When working with data, it's common to organize raw data in one worksheet, perform calculations and analyses in another, and present findings in a third.

Example: A financial analyst might store historical data in one sheet, use another for performing statistical analyses, and present key insights on a final summary sheet.

Tips for Effective Workbook and Worksheet Management

- ❖ *Organize Worksheets Logically*: Group similar data or related topics together to keep your workbook easy to navigate.
- ❖ *Use Descriptive Sheet Names*: Clear, descriptive names for worksheets help you quickly locate the information you need.
- ❖ **Keep Workbooks Lightweight**: Too many worksheets or overly complex workbooks can slow down Excel's performance. Regularly review and optimize your workbooks by removing unnecessary data or consolidating sheets.
- ❖ *Save Your Work Regularly*: Excel provides an autosave function, but it's important to save your work frequently, especially when working with large or complex datasets.

By mastering the concepts of workbooks and worksheets, you'll be able to organize, analyze, and manage your data more effectively in Excel. Understanding how to navigate between sheets, link data across worksheets, and manage workbook components is a crucial skill for performing a wide range of tasks, from budgeting and project management to data analysis and reporting.

3.

Cell Basics: Entering, Editing, and Formatting Data in Cells

In Excel, cells are the basic units where data is stored and manipulated. A good understanding of how to enter, edit, and format data in cells is essential for efficient use of Excel. Here's an expanded guide on each aspect:

Entering Data in Cells

You can enter different types of data into cells, including **text**, **numbers**, **dates**, and **formulas**.

Selecting a Cell:

Click on the cell where you want to enter data. The selected cell is highlighted with a border.

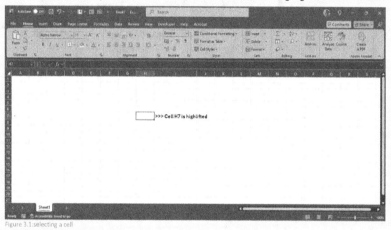

Figure 3.1:selecting a cell

Typing Data:

Start typing to enter your data. It can be:
Text: E.g., "Sales Data"
Numbers: E.g., "1500"
Dates: E.g., "07/02/2025"
Formulas: Start with an equal sign (=), e.g., =SUM(A1:A10).

Completing Data Entry:

Press Enter to confirm and move to the cell directly below, or press Tab to move to the cell to the right. You can also press Esc to cancel data entry.

Editing Data in Cells

Once you've entered data, you may need to make changes. There are two common ways to edit cell data.

Direct Editing:

Click on the cell. Type over the existing data to replace it entirely.

In-cell Editing:

❖ Double-click the cell or press F2 to activate in-cell editing.
❖ The cursor will appear within the cell, allowing you to modify part of the data.

You can also edit the data in the Formula Bar at the top of the screen.

Deleting Data: Select the cell and press the Delete key to remove its content.

Formatting Data in Cells

Formatting helps make your data more readable and presentable. Excel offers various formatting options that apply to text, numbers, and other data types.

Text Formatting:

❖ **Font**: Change the font type, size, and color by selecting the cell, then using the options in the Home tab.
❖ **Bold, Italic, and Underline**: These options can be toggled on and off using the buttons in the Font section.

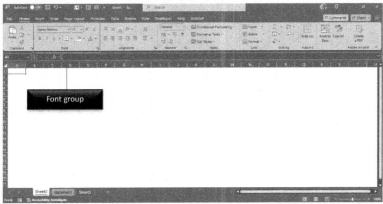

Figure 3.2: Font group

❖ *Alignment*: Align text horizontally (left, center, or right) and vertically (top, middle, or bottom) using the alignment options in the Home tab.

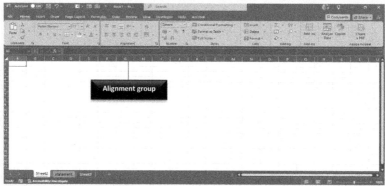

Figure 3.3: Alignment group

Number Formatting:

❖ *General Format*: The default format for numbers.
❖ *Currency*: Displays numbers with currency symbols. E.g., $1,500.00.
❖ *Percentage*: Converts numbers into percentages. E.g., 0.25 becomes 25%.
❖ *Date and Time*: Apply specific formats for dates (e.g., "dd-mm-yyyy") and times.
❖ *Custom Formats*: You can create custom number formats to meet specific requirements.

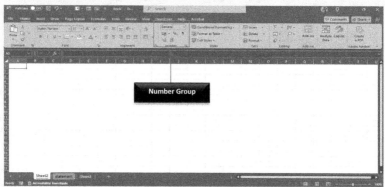

Figure 3.4: Number group

Cell Borders and Fill:

❖ *Borders*: Add or modify borders around cells to visually separate data. Use the border tool in the Font group on home tab
❖ *Fill Color*: Use the Fill Color tool to add background color to cells, helping highlight important data. This feature is in the Font group on home tab
❖ *Wrap Text*: If the content in a cell is too long to fit, use the Wrap Text option to display the content on multiple lines within the cell. This feature is in the alignment group on home tab

❖ **Merge Cells**: Combine multiple cells into one using the Merge & Center option. This is often used for headings. This feature is in the alignment group on home tab
❖ **Conditional Formatting**: You can apply dynamic formatting based on the content of the cells. For example, you could highlight cells with values greater than 1000 in green using Conditional Formatting in the Home tab. This feature can be found in the Style group on Home tab.

By mastering these basic cell operations—entering, editing, and formatting—you'll be able to organize and present your data more effectively in Excel.

4.

Introduction to Basic Formulas and Functions: Learning How to Use Common Functions Like SUM, AVERAGE, and Basic Calculations

Formulas and functions are the backbone of Excel's data manipulation and analysis capabilities. Understanding how to create basic formulas and use common functions is essential for any beginner looking to harness Excel's power. This section will introduce you to some of the most frequently used formulas and functions, such as SUM, AVERAGE, and other basic calculations, to give you a strong foundation for working with data in Excel.

What are Formulas and Functions?

Formulas are expressions used to perform calculations, process data, or retrieve information from cells. They typically start with an equal sign (=), followed by a combination of operators, cell references, values, or functions.

Functions are predefined formulas in Excel designed to perform specific calculations or tasks. They simplify complex operations, so instead of manually writing out a formula, you can use a function to do the work for you.

Key Components:

- ❖ *Cell Reference*: Refers to the value in a specific cell (e.g., A1, B2).
- ❖ *Operators*: Symbols that define the calculation you want to perform (e.g., + for addition, - for subtraction, * for multiplication, / for division).
- ❖ *Function Name*: The name of a predefined function (e.g., SUM, AVERAGE).
- ❖ Arguments: The inputs a function needs to work, typically cell ranges or individual values

---

Basic Formulas in Excel

Basic Arithmetic Operations
Excel allows you to perform basic arithmetic calculations using simple formulas. These operations include addition, subtraction, multiplication, and division.

- ❖ Addition (+): Add numbers or cell values.
  Example: =A1 + B1 adds the values in cells A1 and B1.

- ❖ Subtraction (-): Subtract numbers or cell values.
  Example: =A1 – B1 subtracts the value in B1 from A1.

- ❖ Multiplication (*): Multiply numbers or cell values.
  Example: =A1 * B1 multiplies the values in A1 and B1.

- ❖ Division (/): Divide numbers or cell values.
  Example: =A1 / B1 divides the value in A1 by the value in B1.

These basic formulas can be used in a variety of everyday tasks, such as calculating the total cost of items, tracking expenses, or analyzing numeric data.

Using the SUM Function

The SUM function is one of the most commonly used functions in Excel. It allows you to add together a range of numbers quickly and efficiently.

How to Use SUM:

Syntax: =SUM(number1, [number2], ...)
Number1, number2, etc. can be individual values, cell references, or ranges.

Example 1: Adding a Range of Cells:
If you want to add the values in cells A1 through A5, you would use the formula:
=SUM(A1:A5) This will return the total of all the numbers in those cells.

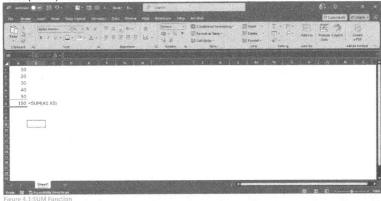

Figure 4.1: SUM Function

Example 2: Adding Multiple Cell References:

You can also sum non-adjacent cells by separating them with commas: =SUM(A1, B1, C1). This will add the values in cells A1, B1, and C1.

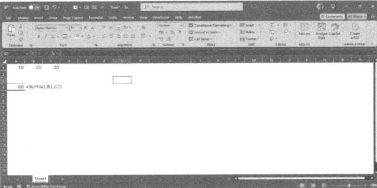

Figure 4.2: Sum of specific cells

Practical Applications:

Budgeting: You can use SUM to add up your total expenses over a period of time.

Inventory Management: Track the total quantity of items across different product categories by summing their counts.

Sales Totals: Calculate the total sales over a week, month, or year by summing daily or monthly sales figures.

Using the AVERAGE Function

The AVERAGE function calculates the arithmetic mean of a set of numbers. This is useful when you want to find the central tendency of a group of numbers.

How to Use AVERAGE:

Syntax: =AVERAGE(number1, [number2], …)
Similar to SUM, number1, number2, etc. can be individual values, cell references, or ranges.

Example 1: Calculating the Average of a Range:

If you want to find the average of values in cells A1 through A5, the formula would be: =AVERAGE(A1:A5)

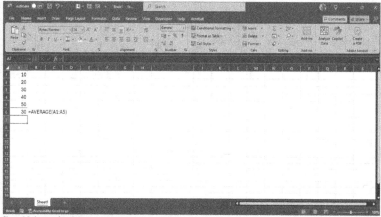

Figure 4.3: Average function

Example 2: Calculating the Average of Specific Cells:
You can calculate the average of non-contiguous cells by listing them in the formula:=AVERAGE(A1, B1, C1)

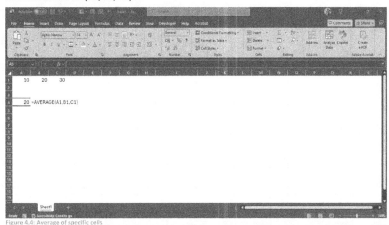

Figure 4.4: Average of specific cells

Practical Applications:

❖ Grade Calculations: Teachers can use AVERAGE to calculate students' average scores across tests or assignments.
❖ Performance Tracking: Businesses can use the function to determine the average sales per day, week, or month.
❖ Personal Finance: Track your average monthly spending or income over a period of time.

Other Common Functions
MIN and MAX Functions:

❖ **MIN**: Returns the smallest number in a range.
  Syntax: =MIN(range)
  Example: =MIN(A1:A10) will return the smallest value in the range A1 to A10.

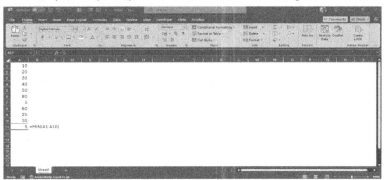

Figure 4.5: Minimum (MIN) function

❖ **MAX**: Returns the largest number in a range.
Syntax: =MAX(range)
Example: =MAX(A1:A10) will return the largest value in the range A1 to A10.

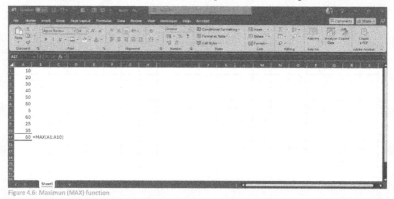

Figure 4.6: Maximun (MAX) function

These functions are helpful when analyzing data to identify outliers, track best/worst performances, or find the extremes in any dataset.

COUNT and COUNTA Functions:

❖ **COUNT**: Counts the number of cells in a range that contain numbers.
Syntax: =COUNT(range)
Example: =COUNT(A1:A10) will count how many cells in the range A1 to A10 contain numerical values.

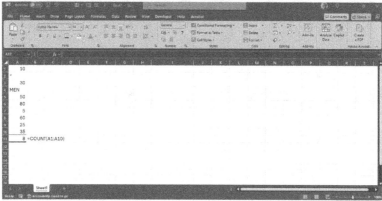

Figure 4.7: Count Function

❖ **COUNTA**: Counts the number of cells in a range that are not empty (including those containing text, numbers, or any other data type).
Syntax: =COUNTA(range)

Example: =COUNTA(A1:A10) will count how many cells in the range A1 to A10 are not empty.

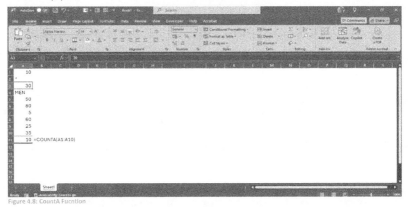

Figure 4.8: CountA Fucntion

IF Function:

The IF function allows you to make logical comparisons between a value and what you expect. It returns one value if a condition is TRUE and another value if it is FALSE.

Syntax: =IF(logical_test, value_if_true, value_if_false)

Example: =IF(A1 > 50, "Pass", "Fail") will return "Pass" if the value in A1 is greater than 50; otherwise, it will return "Fail."

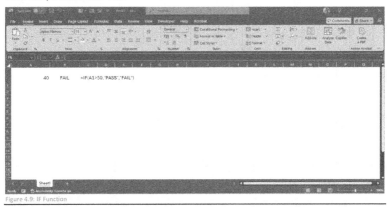

Figure 4.9: IF Function

Best Practices for Using Formulas and Functions:

❖ **Use Cell References:**
   Rather than entering numbers directly into your formulas, it's best to use cell references (e.g.,A1, B2). This allows Excel to automatically update your formulas when the data in the referenced cells changes.

❖ **Copy Formulas with Autofill:**
Excel allows you to copy formulas across multiple cells using the Autofill feature. This is particularly useful for repeating similar calculations across rows or columns.

❖ **Use Parentheses to Control Order of Operations:**
When creating more complex formulas that include multiple operations, use parentheses to ensure the correct order of operations. Excel follows the **_PEMDAS_** rule (Parentheses, Exponents, Multiplication and Division, Addition and Subtraction).
Example: The formula =(A1 + B1) * C1 will add A1 and B1 first, then multiply the result by C1.

❖ **Check for Errors:**
Excel provides several tools to check for errors in your formulas, such as the Formula Auditing toolbar and Error Checking options. Use these tools to identify mistakes like missing references, division by zero, or incorrect ranges.

Practical Exercises to Reinforce Learning

1 **Create a Simple Budget:** Use the SUM function to add up income and expenses, then use basic arithmetic formulas to calculate your savings or balance.
2 **Analyze Test Scores**: Calculate the average of test scores using the AVERAGE function, then use MIN and MAX to find the lowest and highest scores.
3 **Track Product Sales:** Use the COUNT and COUNTA functions to count the number of products sold or track non-empty cells in a sales sheet.

By mastering basic formulas and functions like SUM, AVERAGE, and others, you can perform quick and effective calculations in Excel, making data management more efficient and insightful.

5.

Data Management: Introduction to Sorting, Filtering, and Organizing Data in Excel

Excel is widely used for data management, and being able to sort, filter, and organize data efficiently is essential. These features help you analyze, interpret, and present data more effectively. Below is an expanded guide to these powerful data management tools.

Sorting Data

Sorting allows you to reorder your data based on specific criteria, such as alphabetically, numerically, or by date.

Basic Sorting:

❖ Select the data range or column you want to sort.
❖ Go to the Data tab, then click either Sort Ascending (A to Z) or Sort Descending (Z to A) for text, or Smallest to Largest and Largest to Smallest for numbers.
❖ Excel will automatically adjust the data based on your selection.

Figure 5.1: Basic Sorting

Custom Sorting:

If your data has multiple criteria for sorting (e.g., first by region and then by sales), you can perform a custom sort:

❖ Select your data range.
❖ In the Data tab, click on Sort.
❖ In the Sort dialog box, choose your first criterion (e.g., "Region"), then add levels for additional criteria (e.g., "Sales Amount")
❖ Choose ascending or descending order for each criterion.

Figure 5.2: Custom SOrting

Sorting by Color or Icon:

You can also sort data based on cell color or font color, making it easier to highlight or prioritize certain records.

❖ In the Sort dialog box, choose Cell Color or Font Color under Sort On and specify the order in which the colors should be sorted.

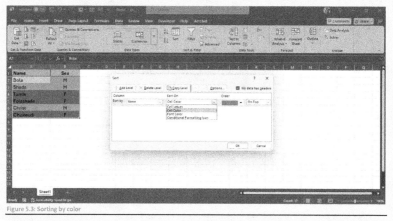

Figure 5.3: Sorting by color

Filtering Data

Filtering allows you to display only the rows that meet certain criteria, making it easier to focus on specific parts of your data.

Basic Filtering:

❖ Select your data range (including headers).
❖ In the Data tab, click on Filter. A drop-down arrow will appear next to each column header.

❖ Click the drop-down arrow in the column where you want to apply a filter and choose the values you want to display.

❖ You can select or deselect specific values or use the search box to quickly find a specific entry.

Figure 5.4: Filter Function

Custom Filters:

In the drop-down menu, click Number Filters (for numbers) or Text Filters (for text) to apply more advanced criteria, such as:

❖ *Equals*: Filter rows with a specific value.

❖ *Does Not Equal*: Filter rows that do not match a specific value.

❖ Greater Than, Less Than: Filter based on numerical values.

❖ Contains, Does Not Contain: Filter based on partial text matches.

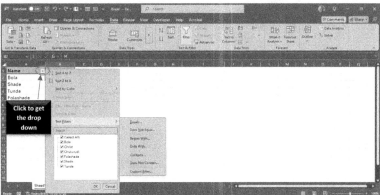

Figure 5.5: Custom Filter

Date Filters:

Excel provides specific filters for dates, such as filtering for records from a particular year, month, week, or even "Last 30 Days" or "Next Month."

Organizing Data

Organizing data effectively in Excel involves structuring and grouping your data in a way that enhances readability and analysis.

Freezing Panes:

Freezing allows you to keep certain rows or columns visible while scrolling through large datasets.

To freeze the first row or column, go to the View tab and click Freeze Panes. You can choose to freeze:

❖ *Top Row*: The first row remains visible as you scroll down.
❖ *First Column*: The first column remains visible as you scroll horizontally.
❖ *Custom Freeze*: Freeze any selected number of rows and columns based on where you place your cursor.

Refer to figure 1.11

Focus cell:

Focus cell was introduced in 2024 and it helps you to focus on a particular cell you have higligthed within a dataset, making it easier to recognise the row and column you are currengly operating on.

❖ In the View tab, go to "show group"
❖ Click on Focus cell.
❖ Move around the dataset

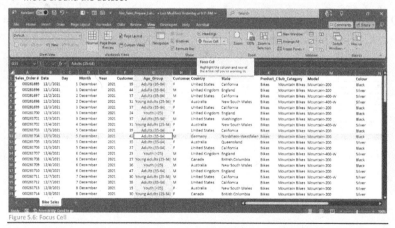

Figure 5.6: Focus Cell

Excel Tables:

Converting your data into an Excel Table makes it easier to manage, as Excel tables come with automatic filtering, sorting, and formatting options.

❖ Select your data and go to the Insert tab, then click Table (or use Ctrl + T).
❖ Tables allow for dynamic ranges (they expand when you add new rows/columns), and each column gets a drop-down filter by default.
❖ You can also apply preset Table Styles to give your data a consistent and professional look.

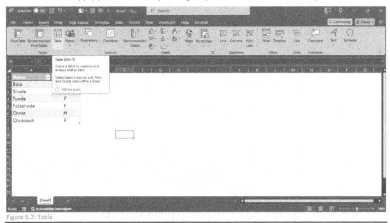

Figure 5.7: Table

Using Data Validation to Organize Data Entry

Data validation helps ensure that only certain types of data are entered into specific   cells.

Creating a Drop-down List:

❖ Select the cells where you want to restrict data entry.
❖ In the Data tab, click Data Validation.
❖ In the Allow box, choose List and enter the allowed values (or refer to a range of values in your worksheet).
❖ This will create a drop-down list, preventing users from entering any values outside the predefined options.

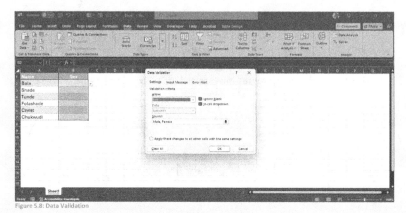

Figure 5.8: Data Validation

Restricting Data Entry:

You can set up rules to ensure only certain types of data are entered, e.g., only numbers within a certain range. In Data Validation, choose from criteria such as whole numbers, decimal numbers, dates, or specific text lengths.

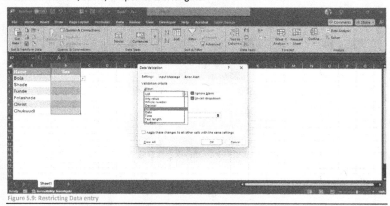

Figure 5.9: Restricting Data entry

Conditional Formatting for Data Organization

Conditional Formatting is a great way to visually organize and emphasize key data points by applying formats such as colors or icons based on cell values.

Applying Conditional Formatting:

❖ Select the range of cells you want to format.
❖ In the Home tab, click Conditional Formatting.
❖ You can apply preset formatting rules, such as highlighting cells greater than a specific value or using a color scale to show higher values in darker shades.

Custom Conditional Formatting:

You can also create custom rules. For example, use a formula to apply formatting, such as coloring rows that meet a specific condition (e.g., =A1>100).

Data Bars and Icon Sets:

Conditional formatting can also be used to insert data bars (colored bars that visually represent the magnitude of a value) or icons (such as checkmarks or warning signs based on conditions).

Figure 5.10: Conditional Formatting

By mastering these data management features in Excel, you'll be able to work with large datasets more effectively, enabling better analysis, decision-making, and presentation. Sorting, filtering, and organizing are foundational tools for anyone working with structured data.

6.

Preliminary Hands-On Exercises: Basic Tasks to Reinforce Learning

As a beginner learning Excel, hands-on exercises are essential for solidifying your understanding of the core concepts. These exercises will help you practice using the Excel interface, formulas, and functions in real-world scenarios. Below are two beginner-friendly tasks: creating a simple budget and a to-do list. Each exercise is designed to build familiarity with essential Excel features like entering data, using basic formulas, and formatting cells to make your work more organized and presentable.

Exercise 1: Creating a Simple Budget

A personal budget is an excellent starting point for Excel learners. It requires basic data entry, the use of simple arithmetic formulas, and organizational skills. You will input income and expenses and then use basic Excel functions to calculate your balance.

Step-by-Step Instructions:

1. *Set Up Your Spreadsheet*:
   Open a new Excel worksheet.
   - ✓ In cell A1, type "Income" and list your income sources below it (e.g., Salary, Freelance, etc.).
   - ✓ In cell B1, type "Amount" and list the corresponding income amounts in column B (e.g., Salary = 3000, Freelance = 500, etc.).
   - ✓ Below your income entries, in cell A6, type "Total Income". Use the SUM function in cell B6 to calculate the total income:
     Formula: =SUM(B2:B5) (assuming B2 to B5 contains your income values).
2. *List Your Expenses*:
   - ✓ In cell A8, type "Expenses" and list your monthly expenses (e.g., Rent, Groceries, Utilities, etc.).
   - ✓ In cell B8, type "Amount" and list the corresponding expense amounts in column B (e.g., Rent = 1000, Groceries = 300, etc.).
   - ✓ Below your expense entries, in cell A14, type "Total Expenses". Use the SUM function in cell B14 to calculate the total expenses:
     Formula: =SUM(B9:B13) (assuming B9 to B13 contains your expense values).
3. *Calculate Your Balance*:
   - ✓ In cell A16, type "Balance".
   - ✓ In cell B16, subtract your total expenses from your total income using a basic subtraction formula:
     Formula: =B6 – B14
4. *Format the Worksheet*:
   - ✓ Bold the headings (Income, Expenses, Total Income, Total Expenses, and Balance) to make them stand out.
   - ✓ Format the currency values (in column B) by selecting the cells and choosing Currency format from the toolbar.

5. *Final Outcome*:
   You now have a simple budget that tracks income, expenses, and calculates your final balance. This exercise helps reinforce the use of basic formulas (SUM, subtraction) and gives you a clear, organized way to manage personal finances in Excel.

Exercise 2: Creating a To-Do List

A to-do list is another simple yet effective way to practice Excel's organizational features. In this exercise, you'll use basic formatting, checkboxes, and simple task management techniques to create a list that tracks tasks and their completion status.

Step-by-Step Instructions:

1. *Set Up Your Spreadsheet*:
   - ✓ Open a new Excel worksheet.
   - ✓ In cell A1, type "Task", and in cell B1, type "Due Date". In cell C1, type "Status".
   - ✓ Below the Task heading, list the tasks you need to accomplish (e.g., Buy groceries, Submit report, Clean house, etc.).
   - ✓ In the Due Date column, enter the deadlines for each task (e.g., 01/15/2025, 01/20/2025).
2. *Add Status and Completion Checkboxes*:
   - ✓ Select column C (Status) where you'll track whether a task is completed or not.
   - ✓ To add checkboxes:
     - Go to the Developer tab (if it's not visible, you can enable it in Excel settings).
     - Click Insert and select the Checkbox from the Form Controls.
     - Place checkboxes in each row of column C (next to each task).
3. *Use Conditional Formatting*:
   - ✓ You can use conditional formatting to make completed tasks stand out (e.g., strike-through or change the text color to grey).
   - ✓ Highlight the task cells (column A) and go to the Home tab, select Conditional Formatting.
   - ✓ Select New rule and under "Rule Type", select Use a formular to determin which cells to format".
   - ✓ In the "format value to determine which cells to format" box, input this formular "=$C:C=true".
   - ✓ Select format and then select the rul based on the check box (e.g. apply strike-through)and click ok.
4. *Calculate Task Progress*:
   - ✓ In cell D1, type "Progress".
   - ✓ Use the COUNTIF function to track how many tasks have been completed. For example, if you have 10 tasks and are using checkboxes in cells C2 to C11:
     Formula: =COUNTIF(C2:C11, TRUE)/COUNTA(A2:A11)
     This formula will calculate the percentage of completed tasks.
   - ✓ Format the Worksheet:
     - Bold the headings (Task, Due Date, Status, and Progress) to make them stand out.
     - Apply borders to your table for a cleaner appearance.
   - ✓ Final Outcome:
     You now have a fully functional to-do list with tasks, due dates, checkboxes for completion, and conditional formatting to track your progress. This exercise

emphasizes Excel's capabilities for task management and helps you practice using conditional formatting and basic formulas.

Additional Hands-On Practice Ideas

1. Personal Monthly Expense Tracker:
   Track your daily or weekly expenses, categorize them (e.g., Food, Transport, Entertainment), and calculate totals for each category using the SUM function.
2. Inventory List:
   Create an inventory sheet to manage items at home or in your small business. Include columns for Item Name, Quantity, and Price. Use formulas to calculate total costs per item and overall inventory value.
3. Simple Gradebook:
   Track student grades using basic formulas like AVERAGE, MIN, and MAX to calculate the class average, highest score, and lowest score.

Key Takeaways from Hands-On Exercises

Practice Makes Perfect: By working through these simple tasks, you'll become more familiar with Excel's basic features like entering data, formatting cells, and using basic functions such as SUM and COUNTIF.

Real-World Applications: The exercises highlight Excel's versatility, showing how it can be used for everyday tasks like budgeting, to-do lists, and more complex tracking and analysis.

Building Confidence: As you complete these exercises, your confidence in navigating Excel will grow, making it easier to tackle more advanced tasks and use additional functions in the future.

These preliminary hands-on exercises will help reinforce the skills learned in the course and set the foundation for more advanced projects.